ONE MORE TIME 3
LET'S HEAR IT FROM THE HEART

CONTENTS

Editor: Cecil Bolton.

First Published 1987
© International Music Publications
Woodford Green
Essex 1G8 8HN

Exclusive Distributors
International Music Publications
Southend Road, Woodford Green,
Essex IG8 8HN, England.

215-2-459

Playing Notes For Automatic Keyboards.

When reading the music and chords in this book, chord symbols or parts of chord symbols shown in brackets should be ignored C(o) C+ and you should continue to play the previous chord.

The following guide will help you select suitable rhythms from those available on your instrument, by referring to the Time Signatures shown at the beginning of each song.

$\frac{6}{8}$ select $\frac{6}{8}$ March or Slow Rock (Fast Speed)

¢ or $\frac{2}{4}$ select $\frac{4}{4}$ March or Swing

C or $\frac{4}{4}$ select Swing Ballad or Foxtrot.

$\frac{3}{4}$ Select Waltz

Sometimes the actual time signature will change during a medley. When this happens, the actual beat will remain constant, but the note values will change. The equivalents are shown over the music ♩ = ♩.

As an example if you are counting 4 crochets to a bar $\frac{4}{4}$ ♩ ♩ ♩ ♩ this can change to two

dotted crochets to a bar $\frac{6}{8}$ ♩. ♩.

Continue counting at the same speed substituting the value of the crochet for a dotted crochet.

| ♩ ♩ ♩ ♩ ‖$\frac{6}{8}$ ♩. ♩. |

The changes of value you will find in this book are given below:-

$\frac{4}{4}$ to $\frac{3}{4}$ ♩ = ♩ $\frac{4}{4}$ to $\frac{6}{8}$ ♩ = ♩.

$\frac{3}{4}$ to $\frac{4}{4}$ ♩ = ♩ $\frac{6}{8}$ to ¢ ♩ = 𝅝

$\frac{6}{8}$ to $\frac{2}{4}$ or $\frac{4}{4}$ (♩. = ♩)

$\frac{2}{4}$ to $\frac{4}{4}$ (♩ = ♩)

Some songs and hymns sound best played out of tempo. This has been indicated on the music. You may of course add a suitable rhythm if you wish.

Adjust the speed control on your instrument to suit each individual medley.

Below, Suggested Registrations are given. These are indicated at the beginning of each medley by one of the letters. (A) to (F).

SUGGESTED REGISTRATIONS

MULTIKEYBOARD		**SINGLE KEYBOARD**
Upper: 16′ 8′ 4′ Flutes: Brass (Trumpet)	(A)	Trumpet: (Brass) Flute
Lower: 8′ 4′ Flutes		
Pedal: 16′ Flute		
Upper: 8′ 4′ Flutes: 8′ String (Tibia)	(B)	Banjo: Flute
Lower: 8′ String		
Pedal: 16′ Flute		
Upper: Brass (Trumpet: Trombone)	(C)	Trumpet: Trombone (Brass)
Lower: 8′ 4′ Flutes: String		
Pedal: 16′ Tuba		
Upper: 8′ 4′ Reeds: 8′ Flute	(D)	Flute: Clarinet (Reed)
Lower: 8′ 4′ Flutes: 8′ String		
Pedal: 16′ Reed		
Upper: 8′ 4′ Flutes: Celeste	(E)	Vibraphone ⎫ Violin (Strings)
Lower: 8′ String		Celeste ⎭
Pedal: 8′ Flute		
Upper: 16′ 8′ 4′ String: 8′ Reed: Piano	(F)	Violin (String) Clarinet (Reed) Piano
Lower: 8′ String: 8′ Flutes		
Pedal: Soft 16′		

Medley 1 Registration: D

I Believe
Climb Ev'ry Mountain
You'll Never Walk Alone

I BELIEVE

Words & Music: Ervin Drake, Irvin Graham,
Jimmy Shirl and Al Stillman

I be-lieve for ev-'ry drop of rain that falls, — a flow-er grows. —

— I be-lieve that some-where in the dark-est night, — a can-dle

glows. ————— I be-lieve for ev-'ry-one who goes a-stray,—

—— some-one will come ————— to show the way. ————

I be-lieve, ——— I be-lieve. I be-lieve a-bove the storm the

small-est pray'r —— will still be heard. ———— I be-lieve that

some-one in the great some-where —— hears ev-'ry word. ———

Ev-'ry time I hear a new born ba-by cry,—— or touch a leaf,—— or see the

sky, ——— Then I know why I be-lieve!

CLIMB EV'RY MOUNTAIN

Words: Oscar Hammerstein 11
Music: Richard Rodgers

Climb ev - 'ry moun - tain, search high and
Climb ev - 'ry moun - tain, ford ev 'ry

low, Fol - low ev - 'ry by - way, ev - 'ry path you
stream, Fol - low ev - 'ry rain - bow, till you find your

know. dream! A dream that will need all the love you can

give, Ev-'ry day of your life for as long as you

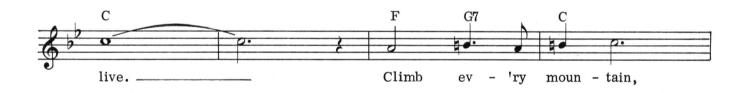

live. Climb ev - 'ry moun - tain,

ford ev - 'ry stream, Fol - low ev - 'ry rain - bow

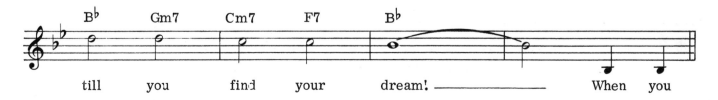

till you find your dream! When you

YOU'LL NEVER WALK ALONE

Words: Oscar Hammerstein 11
Music: Richard Rodgers

Medley 2

Registration: E
Sustained Chords

Abide With Me
The Old Rugged Cross
Amazing Grace
The Lord's My Shepherd

ABIDE WITH ME

Arranged by Chris Ellis and Cecil Bolton

Words: H. F. Lyte
Music: W. H. Monk

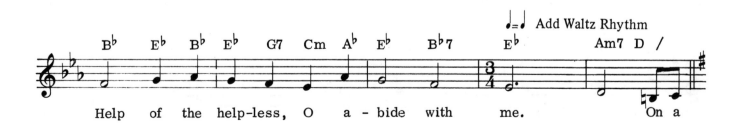

THE OLD RUGGED CROSS

Arranged by Chris Ellis and Cecil Bolton

Words & Music: G. Bennard

© 1987 : International Music Publications, Woodford Green, Essex. 1G8 8HN.

AMAZING GRACE
Arranged by Chris Ellis and Cecil Bolton

Traditional

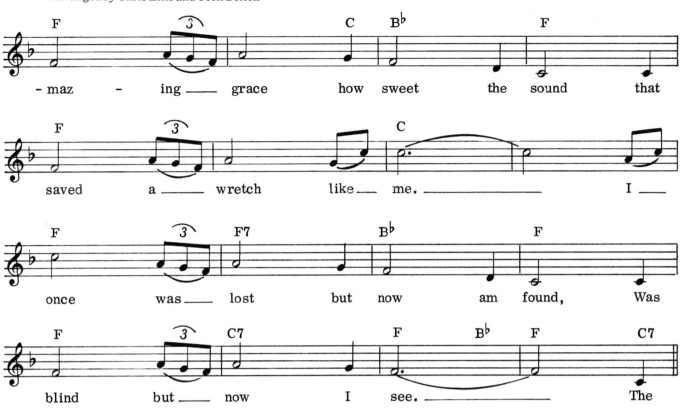

-maz - ing ___ grace how sweet the sound that

saved a ___ wretch like ___ me. _____ I ___

once was ___ lost but now am found, Was

blind but ___ now I see. _____ The

THE LORD'S MY SHEPHERD
Arranged by Chris Ellis and Cecil Bolton

Words: Anon
Music: David Grant

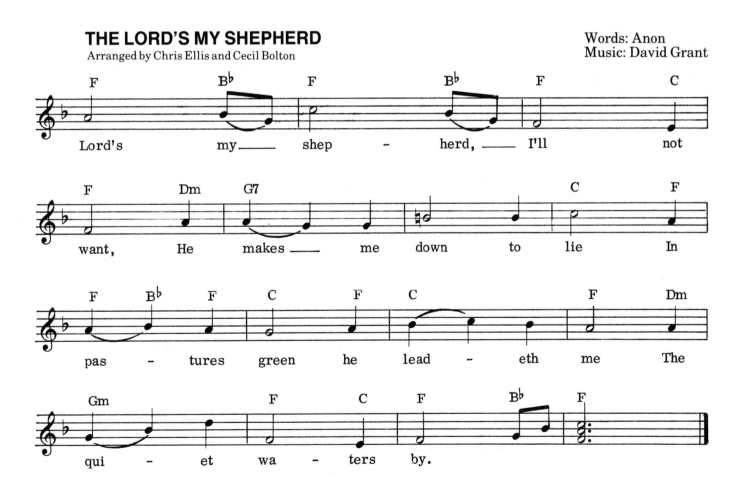

Lord's my ___ shep - herd, ___ I'll not

want, He makes ___ me down to lie In

pas - tures green he lead - eth me The

qui - et wa - ters by.

Medley 3 Registration: C

Jerusalem
To Be A Pilgrim
Onward Christian Soldiers

JERUSALEM

Words & Music: Hubert Parry

Arranged by Chris Ellis and Cecil Bolton

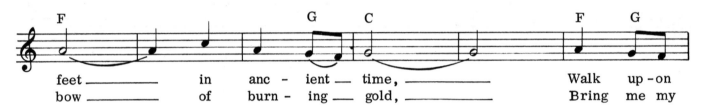

And   did   tho se
Bring   me   my

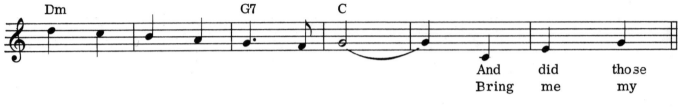

feet ____ in anc - ient __ time, ____ Walk up-on
bow ____ of burn - ing __ gold, ____ Bring me my

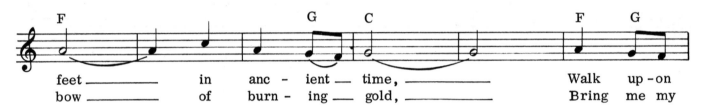

Eng - land's moun - tains green? ____ And was the
ar - rows of de - sire. ____ Bring me my

Ho - ly Lamb of __ God ____ On Eng - land's
spear ____ O clouds un - fold, ____ Bring me my

plea - sant pas - tures seen? ____ And did the Coun -
Char - i - ot of Fire. ____ I will not cease ____

- ten - ance Di - vine ____ Shine forth up - on ____ our
____ from men - tal fight, ____ Nor shall my sword ____ sleep

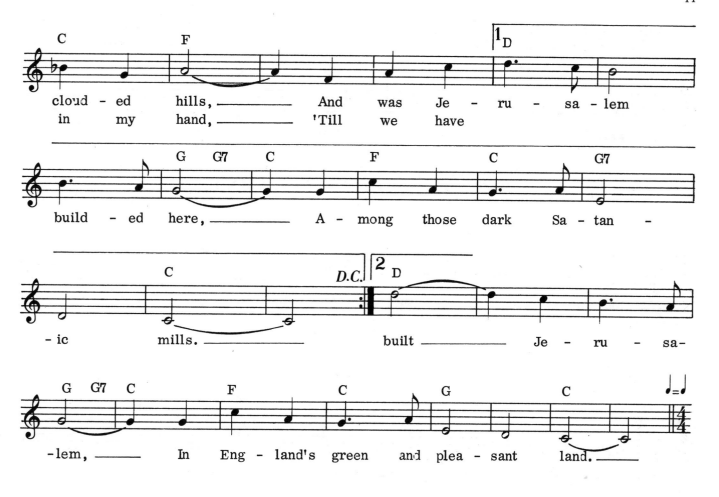

C   F   **1** D

cloud - ed hills, _____ And was Je - ru - sa - lem
in my hand, _____ 'Till we have

G   G7   C   F   C   G7

build - ed here, _____ A - mong those dark Sa - tan -

C   *D.C.* **2** D

- ic mills. _____ built _____ Je - ru - sa -

G   G7   C   F   C   G   C

-lem, _____ In Eng - land's green and plea - sant land. _____

TO BE A PILGRIM

Arranged by Chris Ellis and Cecil Bolton

Words: John Bunyon
Music: Traditional

C   G   C   F   G   C   G   C

He _____ who would val - i - ant be, 'Gainst all di - sas - ter.

C   G   C   F   G   C   G   C

Let _____ him in con - stan - cy, Fol - low the Mast - er.

C   Am   Em   F   G7   C   C   Dm   C   G7

There's no dis - cour - age - ment, _____ Shall make him once re - lent, _____

C   F   Dm   C   G   C

_____ His first a - vowed _ in - tent To be a pil - grim. _____

ONWARD CHRISTIAN SOLDIERS
Arranged by Chris Ellis and Cecil Bolton

Words: S. Baring-Gould
Music: Sir Arthur Sullivan

On - ward Christ-ian Sol - diers, March-ing as to war,

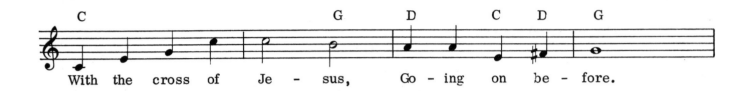

With the cross of Je - sus, Go - ing on be - fore.

Christ, the roy - al mas - ter, Leads a - gainst the foe;

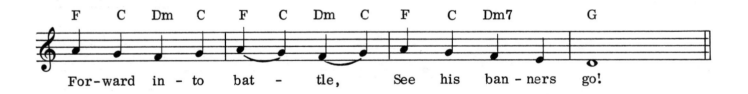

For-ward in - to bat - tle, See his ban - ners go!

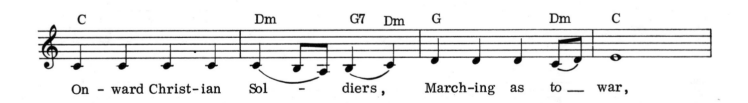

On - ward Christ-ian Sol - diers, March-ing as to __ war,

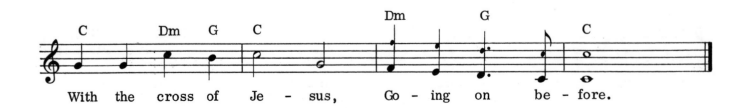

With the cross of Je - sus, Go - ing on be - fore.

Medley 4

Registration: E
Sustained Chords

Bless This House
At The End Of The Day
The Day Thou Gavest

BLESS THIS HOUSE

Words: Helen Taylor
Music: May H. Brahe

AT THE END OF THE DAY

Words & Music: Donald O'Keefe

Add Waltz Rhythm

At the end of the day Just kneel and say, "Thank you Lord for my work and play, I've tried to be good, For I know that I should," That's my prayer for the end of the day. The

THE DAY THOU GAVEST

Words: J. Ellerton
Music: C. Scholefield

Arranged by Chris Ellis and Cecil Bolton

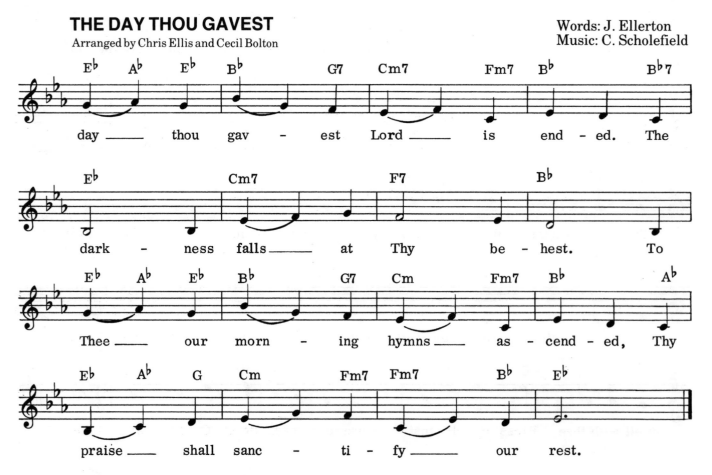

day thou gav - est Lord is end - ed. The dark - ness falls at Thy be - hest. To Thee our morn - ing hymns as - cend - ed, Thy praise shall sanc - ti - fy our rest.

Medley 5

Registration: F
Sustained Chords

The Lost Chord
The Holy City
Hallelujah Chorus (Theme)

THE LOST CHORD

Arranged by Chris Ellis and Cecil Bolton

Words: A. A. Proctor
Music: Sir Arthur Sullivan

THE HOLY CITY

Arranged by Chris Ellis and Cecil Bolton

Words: F. Weatherly
Music: Stephen Adams

-ru - sa-lem Je - ru - sa-lem, Lift up your gates and sing. Ho-

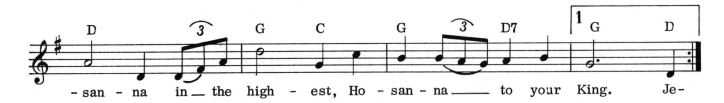

-san - na in the high - est, Ho - san - na to your King. Je-

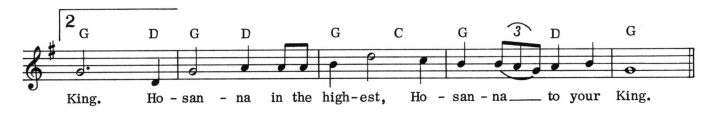

King. Ho - san - na in the high-est, Ho - san - na to your King.

© 1987 : International Music Publications, Woodford Green, Essex. 1G8 8HN.

HALLELUJAH CHORUS (Theme)

Arranged by Chris Ellis and Cecil Bolton

Words & Music: G. F. Handel

Hal - le - lu - jah, Hal - le - lu-jah, Hal-le - lu-jah, Hal-le-lu-jah, Hal-

le - lu - jah. Hal - le - lu - jah, Hal - le - lu - jah, Hal-le-

-lu - jah, Hal-le-lu-jah, Hal - le - lu - jah. For the Lord

God om-ni - po - tent reign - eth, Hal -le - lu-jah, Hal - le -lu-jah, Hal-le-

© 1987 : International Music Publications, Woodford Green, Essex. 1G8 8HN.

Medley 6

Registration: C
Sustained Chords

Eternal Father Strong To Save
Rock Of Ages
Oh God Our Help In Ages Past

ETERNAL FATHER STRONG TO SAVE

Arranged by Chris Ellis and Cecil Bolton

Words: W. Whiting
Music: J. Dykes

E -

-ter - nal Fa - ther strong to save, Whose arm hath bound the

rest - less wave, Who bidd'st the migh - ty o - cean deep Its

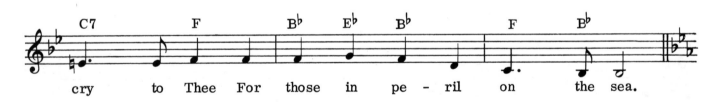

own ap - point - ed li - mits keep: O Hear us when we

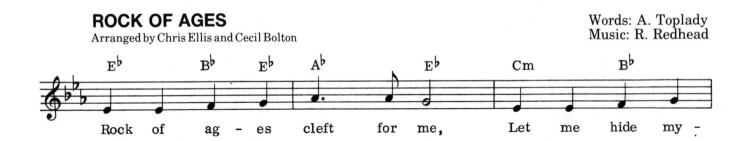

cry to Thee For those in pe - ril on the sea.

ROCK OF AGES

Arranged by Chris Ellis and Cecil Bolton

Words: A. Toplady
Music: R. Redhead

Rock of ag - es cleft for me, Let me hide my -

-self in thee. Let the wat - er and the blood

From thy riv - en side which flowed, Be of sin the

dou - ble cure: Cleanse me from its guilt and power.

O GOD OUR HELP IN AGES PAST

Arranged by Chris Ellis and Cecil Bolton

Words: I. Watts
Music: W. Croft

O God our help in a - ges past, Our

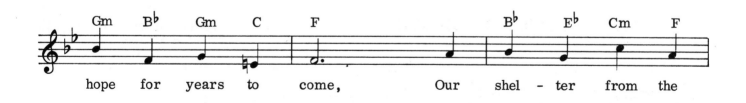

hope for years to come, Our shel - ter from the

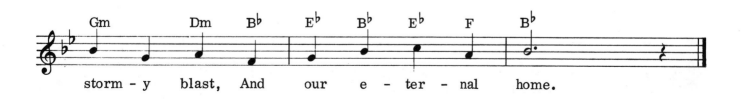

storm - y blast, And our e - ter - nal home.

Medley 7

Registration: A
Sustained Chords

All People That On Earth Do Dwell
Now Thank We All Our God
Praise The Lord Ye Heavens Adore Him

ALL PEOPLE THAT ON EARTH DO DWELL

Arranged by Chris Ellis and Cecil Bolton

Words: W. Kethe
Music: L. Bourgeoise

All

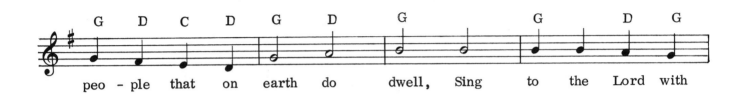

peo - ple that on earth do dwell, Sing to the Lord with

cheer - ful voice, Him serve with fear his praise forth -

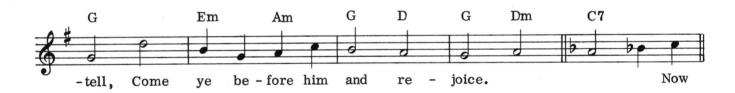

-tell, Come ye be - fore him and re - joice.

Now

NOW THANK WE ALL OUR GOD

Arranged by Chris Ellis and Cecil Bolton

Words: Catherine Winkworth
Music: J. Cruger

thank we all our God with heart and hands and voi - ces. _____ Who

won-'drous things have done In whom His world re - joi - ces. _____ Who

from our moth-er's arms Hath blessed_us on our way With

count-less gifts of love, And still is ours to - day.

PRAISE THE LORD YE HEAVENS ADORE HIM

Arranged by Chris Ellis and Cecil Bolton

Words: J. Kempthorne
Music: J. Haydn

Praise the Lord, ye heavens, a - dore_ him; Praise him, an - gels,

in the_ height; Sun and moon, re - joice be - fore_ him,

Praise him, all ye stars and _ light. Praise the Lord,_ for

he hath spo - ken; Worlds his migh - ty voice o - beyed.

Laws, which nev - er shall be bro - ken, For their guid - ance

he hath _ made.

Medley 8 Registration: C

Land Of Our Fathers
Men Of Harlech
We'll Keep A Welcome

LAND OF OUR FATHERS
Arranged by Chris Ellis and Cecil Bolton

Words: Anon
Music: James James

Oh!

land of my fa - thers, the land of the — free, The

home of the Tel - yn so sooth - ing to me. Thy

no - ble de - fend - ers were — gall - ant and — brave, For

free - dom their heart's life they gave. ____

Wales, Wales, home, ____ sweet home ____ is

Wales, ____ 'Til death be — passed my love shall—

last, My long - ing, my yearn - ing for Wales.

MEN OF HARLECH

Arranged by Chris Ellis and Cecil Bolton

Welsh Traditional

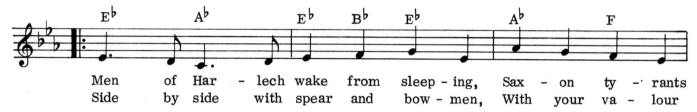

Men of Har - lech wake from sleep - ing, Sax - on ty - rants
Side by side with spear and bow - men, With your va - lour

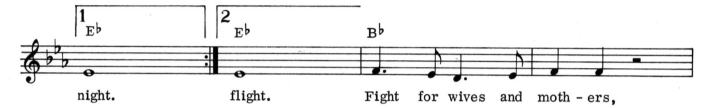

now are creep - ing, Like a riv - er on - ward sweep-ing, Swift - ly thru' the
you shall show men, How to van - quish Sax - on foe-men, Put them all to

night.   flight.   Fight for wives and moth - ers,

Child - ren sis - ters broth-ers, Your count - ry needs your gal - lant deeds To

save _ your - self _ and _ oth - ers, Whilst the bat - tle drums are beat - ing,

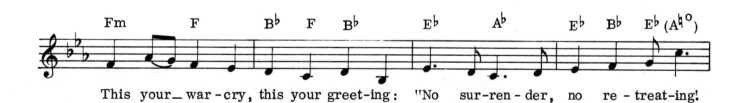

This your _ war - cry, this your greet-ing: "No sur-ren - der, no re - treat-ing!

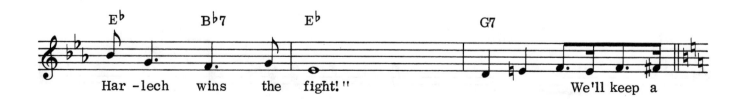

Har - lech wins the fight!"   We'll keep a

WE'LL KEEP A WELCOME

Words: Lyn Joshua and James Harper
Music: Mai Jones

wel - come in the hill - side, _____ We'll keep a wel - come in the

vales, _____ This land you knew will still be sing - ing _____ When you come

home a - gain to Wales, _____ This land of song will keep a

wel - come, _____ And with a love that nev - er fails, _____ Will kiss a -

-way each hour of Hir - aeth, When you come home a - gain to

Wales, _____ Will kiss a - way each hour of Hir - eath, When you

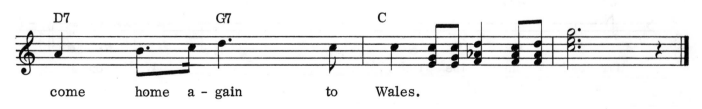

come home a - gain to Wales.

Medley 9 Registration: B

It's A Long Way To Tipperary
There's A Long Long Trail
Keep The Home Fires Burning
Pack Up Your Troubles

IT'S A LONG WAY TO TIPPERARY

Words & Music: Jack Judge & Harry Williams

It's a long way — to Tip-per--ar-y, It's a long way to go. It's a long way — to Tip-per--ar-y, To the sweet-est girl I know. Good-bye Pic-ca--dil-ly, fare-well Leices-ter Square, It's a long long way to Tip-per--ar-y, But my heart's right there. There's a

THERE'S A LONG LONG TRAIL

Words & Music: Stoddard King and Zo Elliott

long, long trail a - wind-ing — in-to the land of my dreams, Where the night - in-gales are sing-ing and the white moon beams: There's a long, long night of wait-ing — un-til my dreams all come true: 'Til the day when I'll be go - ing down that long, long trail — with you.

KEEP THE HOME FIRES BURNING

Words: Lena Guilbert Ford
Music: Ivor Novello

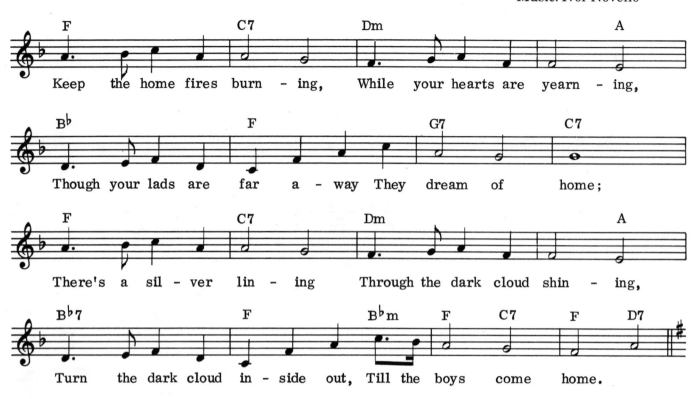

Keep the home fires burn - ing, While your hearts are yearn - ing,
Though your lads are far a - way They dream of home;
There's a sil - ver lin - ing Through the dark cloud shin - ing,
Turn the dark cloud in - side out, Till the boys come home.

PACK UP YOUR TROUBLES

Words: George Asaf
Music: Felix Powell

Pack up your trou-bles in your old kit bag and smile, smile,
smile. While there's a luc - i - fer to light your fag,
smile boys, that's the style. What's the use of wor-ry-ing, It
nev - er was worth - while, So pack up your trou-bles in your
old kit bag and smile, smile, smile. ____

Medley 10 Registration: C

There'll Always Be An England
I Vow To Thee My Country
Song Of Liberty
Land Of Hope And Glory

THERE'LL ALWAYS BE AN ENGLAND

Words & Music: Ross Parker
& Hughie Charles

I VOW TO THEE MY COUNTRY
Arranged by Chris Ellis and Cecil Bolton

Words: Sir Cecil Spring-Rice
Music: Gustav Holst

Vow to Thee my coun-try all earth-ly things a-bove. En-
-tire and whole and per-fect the ser-vice of my love. The —
love that asks no ques-tions, The — love that stays the test, That —
looks up-on the al-ter, the dear-est and the best. The —
love that nev-er fal-ters, The love that pays the price. The —
love that makes un-daun-ted the fi-nal sac-ri-fice.

SONG OF LIBERTY

Words: A. P. Herbert
Music: Edward Elgar

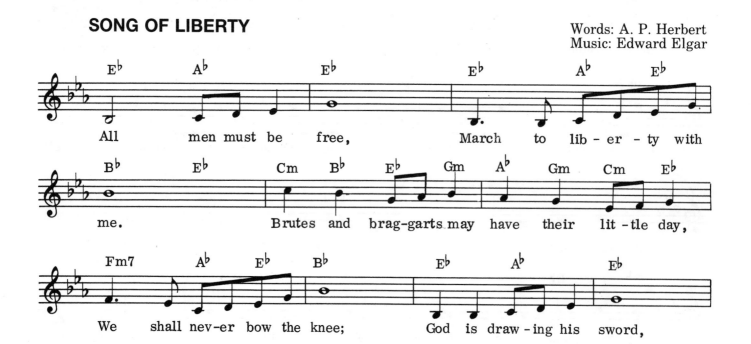

All men must be free, March to lib-er-ty with
me. Brutes and brag-garts may have their lit-tle day,
We shall nev-er bow the knee; God is draw-ing his sword,

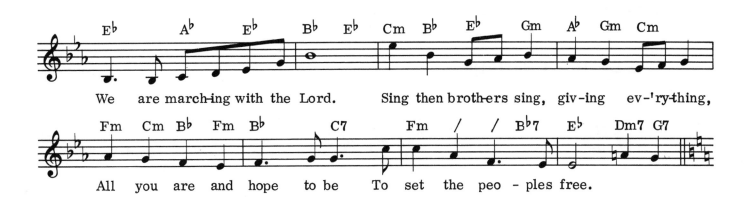

We are march-ing with the Lord. Sing then broth-ers sing, giv-ing ev-'ry-thing,

All you are and hope to be To set the peo - ples free.

LAND OF HOPE AND GLORY

Arranged by Chris Ellis and Cecil Bolton

Words: A. C. Benson
Music: Edward Elgar

Land of hope and glo - ry, Mo-ther of the free.

How shall we ex - tol thee, who are born of thee?

Wi - der still and wi - der shall thy bounds be set;

God, who made thee might - y, make thee might - ier yet;

God, who made thee might - y, make thee might - ier yet.

make thee might ier yet.

Medley 11 Registration: A

The British Grenadiers
Sons Of The Sea
Hearts Of Oak
Soldiers Of The Queen
Rule Britannia

THE BRITISH GRENADIERS

Traditional

Arranged by Chris Ellis and Cecil Bolton

Some

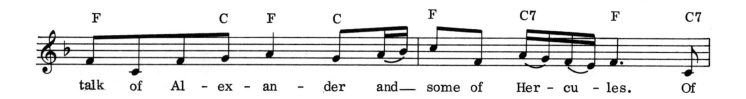

talk of Al - ex - an - der and — some of Her - cu - les. Of

Hec - tor and Ly - san - der And — such great names — as — these. But of

all the world's brave he - ros there's none that can — com - pare, With a

Tow - row — row row — row row — row to the Bri - tish Gre - na - diers.

SONS OF THE SEA

Words & Music: Felix McGlennon

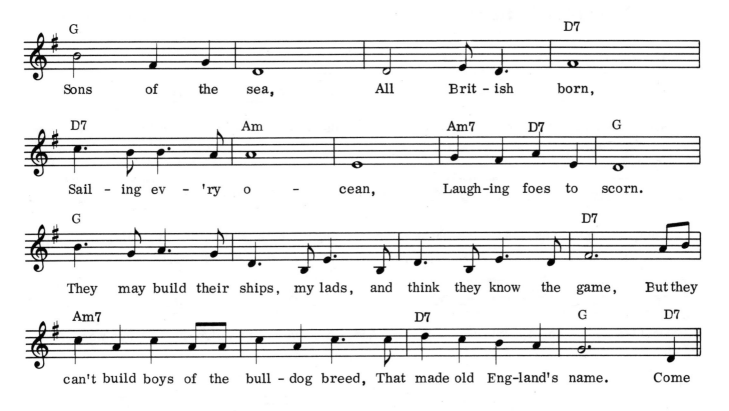

Sons of the sea, All Brit - ish born, Sail - ing ev - 'ry o - cean, Laugh-ing foes to scorn. They may build their ships, my lads, and think they know the game, But they can't build boys of the bull - dog breed, That made old Eng-land's name. Come

HEARTS OF OAK

Traditional

Arranged by Chris Ellis and Cecil Bolton

cheer up my lads, 'tis to glo - ry we steer, To add some-thing new to this won - der-ful year, To — hon - our we call you, not press you like slaves, For who are so free as the sons of the waves. Heart of Oak are our ships, Jol - ly tars are our men, We al-ways are rea-dy, Stea-dy, boys stea-dy, We'll fight and we'll con-quer a--gain and a - gain. It's the

SOLDIERS OF THE QUEEN
Arranged by Chris Ellis and Cecil Bolton

Words & Music: Leslie Stuart

Sol - diers of the Queen, my lads, Who've been, my lads, Who've seen, my lads, In the fight for Eng - land's glo - ry, lads, Of its world-wide glo - ry let us sing. And when we say we've al - ways won, And when they ask us how it's done, We'll proud - ly point to ev - 'ry one Of Eng - land's Sol - diers of the Queen.

RULE BRITANNIA
Arranged by Chris Ellis and Cecil Bolton

Traditional

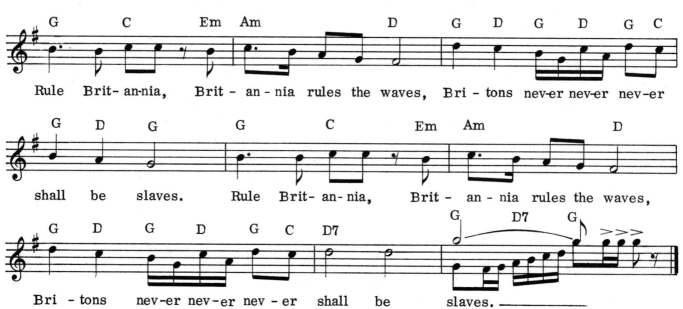

Rule Brit - an-nia, Brit - an - nia rules the waves, Bri - tons nev-er nev-er nev-er shall be slaves. Rule Brit - an-nia, Brit - an - nia rules the waves, Bri - tons nev-er nev-er nev - er shall be slaves.

Medley 12 Registration: F

A Gordon For Me
Loch Lomond
The Campbells Are Coming
With A Hundred Pipers
Keep Right On To The End Of The Road

A GORDON FOR ME

Words & Music: Robert Wilson

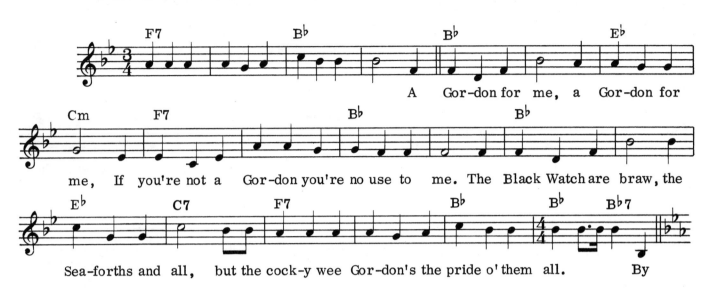

A Gor-don for me, a Gor-don for me, If you're not a Gor-don you're no use to me. The Black Watch are braw, the Sea-forths and all, but the cock-y wee Gor-don's the pride o' them all. By

LOCH LOMOND

Traditional

Arranged by Chris Ellis and Cecil Bolton

yon bon - nie banks and by yon bon - nie braes, Where the sun shines bright on Loch Lo - mond, Where me and my true love were ev - er wont to gae, On the bon-nie, bon-nie banks of Loch Lo - mond. O, you'll tak' the high road, and I'll tak' the low road, And I'll be in Scot - land a - fore ye; But me and my true love will nev-er meet a - gain, On the bon-nie bon-nie banks of Loch- Lo - mond. The

THE CAMPBELLS ARE COMING

Arranged by Chris Ellis and Cecil Bolton

Traditional

WITH A HUNDRED PIPERS

Arranged by Chris Ellis and Cecil Bolton

Traditional

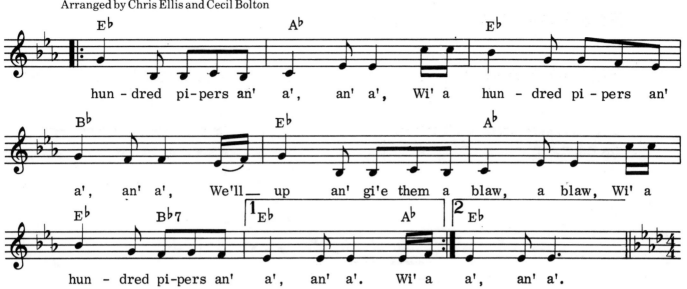

hun - dred pi-pers an' a', an' a', Wi' a hun - dred pi - pers an'
a', an' a', We'll up an' gi'e them a blaw, a blaw, Wi' a
hun - dred pi-pers an' a', an' a'. Wi' a a', an' a'.

KEEP RIGHT ON TO THE END OF THE ROAD

Words & Music:
William Dillon & Harry Lauder

Keep right on to the end of the road, Keep right on to the
end. Tho' the way be long let your heart be strong,
Keep right on round the bend. Tho' you're tired and wea-ry,
Still jour - ney on, Till you come to that hap-py a - bode, Where
all the love you've been dream-ing of will be there at the
end of the road.

Medley 13

Registration: E
Sustained Chords

Galway Bay
The Mountains Of Mourne
Danny Boy

GALWAY BAY

Words & Music: Dr. Arthur Colahan

If you ev-er go a-cross the sea to Ire-land, Then may-be at the clos-ing of your day, You will sit and watch the moon rise o-ver Clad-dagh, And see the sun go down on Gal-way Bay. Just to hear a-gain the rip-ple of the trout stream, The wo-men in the mea-dows mak-ing hay, And to sit be-side a turf fire in the cab-in, And watch the bare-foot Gos-soons at their play, And if there is going to be a life here-af-ter, And some-how I am sure there's going to be, I will ask my God to let me make my hea-ven, In that dear land a-cross the I-rish sea. Oh

Published by Permission of Pigott & Co. Ltd., 112, Grafton Street, Dublin.
© 1947 : Box & Cox (Publications), 44 Seymour Place, London, W1H 5WQ.

THE MOUNTAINS OF MOURNE
Words & Music: Percy French and Houston Collisson
Arranged by Chris Ellis and Cecil Bolton

DANNY BOY

Arranged by Chris Ellis and Cecil Bolton

Words: E. Weatherly
Music: Irish Traditional

Medley 14 Registration: B

Blaze Away
The Happy Wanderer

BLAZE AWAY

Words: Jimmy Kennedy
Music: Abe Holzmann

THE HAPPY WANDERER

Words: Antonia Ridge
Music: Friedr. W. Moller

Medley 15 Registration: C

For He's A Jolly Good Fellow
Viva La Company
Good Night Ladies
Auld Lang Syne

FOR HE'S A JOLLY GOOD FELLOW

Traditional

Arranged by Chris Ellis and Cecil Bolton

For _____ he's a jol - ly good fel - low, For

he's a jol - ly good fel - low, For he's a jol - ly good

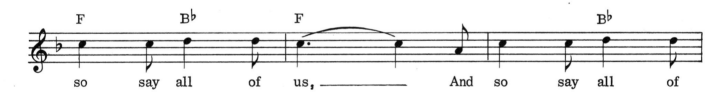

fel - low, And so say all of us. _____ And

so say all of us, _____ And so say all of

us; _____ For he's a jol - ly good fel - low, For

he's a jol - ly good fel - low, For he's a jol - ly good

fel - low, And so say all of us.

VIVA LA COMPANY
Arranged by Chris Ellis and Cecil Bolton

Traditional

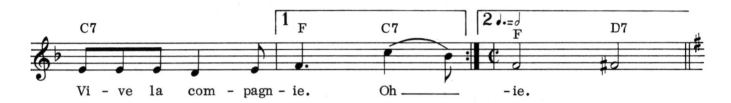

GOOD NIGHT LADIES
Arranged by Chris Ellis and Cecil Bolton

Traditional

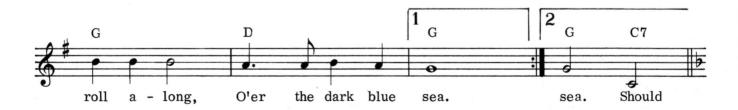

AULD LANG SYNE

Arranged by Chris Ellis and Cecil Bolton

Traditional

Medley 16 Registration: A

Eton Boating Song
Whiffenpoof Song
The Stein Song

ETON BOATING SONG

Words: William Johnson Cory
Music: Algernon Drummond and Evelyn Wodehouse

Jol - ly boat - ing wea - ther, And a hay har - vest breeze. Blade on the fea - ther, Shade off the trees. Swing, swing to - geth - er, With your backs be- -tween your knees, Swing, swing to - geth - er, With your backs be- -tween your knees. We are

THE WHIFFENPOOF SONG

Words & Music: Meade Minnigerode, George S. Pomeroy
& Tod B. Galloway   Revision By: Rudy Vallee

THE STEIN SONG

Words: Chas. S. Adelman and I. Blumenstock
Music: Ben Jerome

Fill _____ the steins for auld lang syne,

Shout till the raft - ers ring, _____

Stand _____ and drink a toast once a - gain, _____ Let

ev - 'ry loy - al voice now sing. _____ Then

drink _____ to all the hap - py hours,

Drink to the care - less days, _____

Drink _____ to all who may be ab - sent, _____ Yet

lin - ger in our hearts al - ways.